Overtime
and
The Dance

Michael D. Jones

Grey Wolfe Publishing, LLC
PO Box 1088
Birmingham, Michigan 48009
www.GreyWolfePublishing.com

© 2016; 2017 Michael D. Jones
Published by Grey Wolfe Publishing, LLC
www.GreyWolfePublishing.com
All Rights Reserved

First Edition ISBN: 978-1628281798
Second Edition ISBN: 978-1628281828
Library of Congress Control Number: 2016960472

Grey Wolfe Publishing LLC
Uí bóna na corbín

Overtime
and
The Dance

Michael D. Jones

Dedication

To Chris and Cathy, my brother and sister.

Acknowledgements

Cover art, "Insight; One Moment in Time" by David Grant Roth, is used with the permission of his estate (Bonnie Barton Roth).

I would also like to acknowledge the editors of the following, where early versions of these poems appeared for the first time:

The *Kerf 2015*; "Ambersong" (Pushcart Prize nominee).

Legends Literary Journal 2015; "Inspired by an Elegy", "Late Winter Ice, Storm", "North Texas Rain", "Of Overtime and the Beginning", "Overtime and The Dance", "Round Trip/Ode to a Massage Chair", and "The Emergent Poet at Fifty".

The Garfield Lake Review 2015; "Aliens and Zombies", "Ausonius at Moselle", "More Whiskey Please", "On Leaving Little Traverse", *"Overtime and Charley", "Overtime and Golf", "Overtime Celebrates", and *"Overtime Gets Real" (formerly Overtime #2, #3, #4, and #5).

Third Wednesday 2016; "Overtime, The Moon, The End, and Us" and "Of Overtime and Endings".

Contents

I.

II.

III.

I.

Ausonius at Moselle
Decimus Magnus Ausonius, 310-395 A.D.

The long Virgilian lines
Could not hold Ausonius'
Beloved Moselle (no matter
How clear, or how well crafted
Their immutable spirit) and sense
Of his last days. So, I translate
"Descending quickly now
Across the river, mist
Invades, overwhelming
The ancient walls of Vincum
Where Gaulish Latium
Succumbed and scattered lay
Abandoned on the battlefield."
Such is decline that only
In retrospect, uprisings seem
Like lemon sorbet between
Courses to cleanse the palette
At your lavish Bordeaux estate-
The hillside vineyards ripe
For picking, river trout at rest
In shaded pools, the colonies
Of tended bees in their swollen
Hives, unaware the Limes
Are broken- no longer keeping
The barbarians among us out.
Soon, the harvest will come.
The harvest feast will come.

Of Overtime and The Beginning

Once the beginning began, Overtime
which is both within and beyond all time
invisibly stirred among the cooling stars
like dark matter adding weight to the Universe
(as if Time's slow tick didn't weigh enough).
So when Time first smiled and crawled
for the camera, Overtime leaned waiting
the patient twin unseen against the outer edge.
And when Time first cried out in the void
Overtime moved with compassion, answered
Whaaaa... with *...ahhhh* in the near distance
(Overtime never echoes and always answers).
So, when the Creator first willed the darkness
into light and brought forth rules for the game
Time and Overtime had already doped it out-
Time, in all its authority and majestic splendor
would have its day, and Overtime all the rest
(which is both within and beyond all time
over time). The beginning began once
with stirring breath, divining spark, weight.

Overtime Celebrates

As with all good sports, Overtime
enters like a caterer balancing platters
well before the guests arrive while
your hair is still wet, the kids
are half dressed, the dog conflicted
runs out the open door and back in
where the platters (remember platters?)
are heaped with the most delicious
Whatevers, and bottles jingle your
National Anthem on the white table
where glasses stand, sway, and sing.
Try telling me any dinner party
isn't a competition, or even a Sunday
brunch for your average American
family of four doesn't qualify as
good sport. *He who eats fastest
eats most*, as the saying goes. Or,
as the Carey brothers breaking bread
often carry on- *Let's fight about it.*
Try telling me over coffee and desert
then an aperitif, and another, another
accumulating, rising like bubbles
until the balance shifts, then napkins
drift, pigs-in-a-blanket fly, toothpicks
cascade. Glasses sing Auld Lang Syne.
As with all good sports, Overtime
exits when the hunger and fighting end.

The After Party

The louder party in a brighter room
Where everyone half-dressed in finery
Revels- shouts and drinks and dances-
Knees wobble, hips swing, eyes avert
Or not. *What?*
                      I can barely hear you.
Forgive me, but you don't look so good
After a long night carousing, my dear
And I too must show signs of wear
And couldn't write a decent sonnet
To save my life. Something about
The prevalence of euphemisms when
Everything worthwhile has been said.
Still the band plays on,
                      so we dance.

Overtime's Cartography

Overtime's cartography unfolds beyond the page
unknowingly confident- as if with an assuring nod
characteristic of drunk uncles and newborns
fearlessly grants permission to abandon all reason
and go beyond our constructed and artificial limits
in seeking St. Brendan's Isle of the Blessed, or
with mad determination and unbridled passion
like exiled Viking explorers (Erik the Red or Leif)
in search of new homelands, rumored green lands
willfully fabricated out of transcendent need
for better foods, direct routes to India's spice
past the Persian ports with Eudoxus of Cyzicus
or like wayward Phoenician sailors to colonize
undiscovered countries, untranslatable frontiers.
So Pythagoras first theorized perception's horizon
was sufficiently short sighted, and relied on linear
extrapolations to travel beyond the outstretched
popular concept that our world is flat like the map
Ptolemy drew, Su Song printed, Marco Polo sailed.
Then Pope Sixtus IV envisioned, von Behaim built
Magellan (gone 'round the bend) circumnavigated
this distracted globe where Overtime holds a seat
remembering ghostlike and ubiquitous places
it never traveled, girds the spirits of Cartographers
and madmen adventurers as they strap themselves
to mast and rocket, point at stars and far horizons
with thick and steady hands on tiller and telescope
riding the verdant shallows and cobalt blue depths
their gaze cast wide, the sextant measured distance
in darkness like wakeful dreams, bold imaginings
reshaping our understanding of each misperception
unknowingly confident, as if with an assuring nod.
Overtime's cartography unfolds beyond the page
As we enlarge the world, extending written lines.

Round Trip
GRR to Palm Coast

For eight long minutes you made me forget.
Yes, inches of early dark lake effect snow
Left me in 32B while runway plows cleared
And the self-absorbed fumed their poison
Let me off now's and *I don't care about's*
For over two hours, you have no idea my
Beloved massage chair, how demeaning
(Demean: Latin; drive animals) yes, demeaning
Flying coach in Winter is; being packed in
Jostled, stifled, and compressed. Yes, you
Made me forget I missed my connection
In Cincinnati where air marshals arrested
Some hooded punk outside my gate. Yes
You squeezed my cramped Seat E memories
Of XXL brothers who thought I'd move. Yes
You chopped away my second flight delay
Waiting on a new part for the cockpit. Yes
You effleuraged my re-route in Atlanta
After missing a second Jacksonville flight
Which by this point, I almost did not mind-
Why not Daytona in November en route
To Palm Coast? It is half an hour closer
To my aged Eighty-Seven year old father
Who no longer travels or says, *Yes.* You
Were set in Concourse F just for me; yes
Destined to meet on my return flight. Yes
You kneaded my tired calves, knees, thighs
My gluteus, *oh*, rocked my aching hips, *oh*,
Firmly rolled your way up my back. Oh, yes
My massage chair, like a snake charmer you
Relaxed muscle groups and aligned my spine
Cleared my mind; *Yes,* I give you, *Thanks.*
I tingled after the vibrations stopped, walking
To my next gate. The best dollar I ever spent.

Ode to a Massage Chair
Concourse F, Minneapolis-St. Paul International Airport

For eight long minutes you made me forget.
Yes,

                        , you

                                    yes,
                            ;
                                . Yes, you

                                        . Yes
You
                                            . Yes
You
                                            . Yes
You

                                            .

            ?

                                    , *Yes*. You
                                        ; yes.
                                        . Yes
You
                , *oh*,   , *oh*,
                                        . Oh, yes
                                            you

            ; *Yes*,   you, *Thanks*.

            . The best dollar I ever spent.

Holland Lakeshore Fogbank

Grey off the big lake, late spring
                                 granular fog
Not mist- not small drops that hang and stick
But inherent wet on sidewalk and road, slick
As if water could invisibly rise up through
Or weep from stone,
                         even my bare skin clams
With creeping cold damp. *Little cats feet my ass*
More like a lost army, silently marching
Weaving and flowing through thickening trees
Their leaves riffling wildly, limbs pushed aside
By grey, liquid hands.
                       I am compelled to watch
The breadth and breath of fogbank that lingers
Among the trees, it's billowing shroud enfolds
My world this sunless morning
                         until the last wisp
Vanishes into thinly clouded heights and is gone
Ghostly and naturally divine-
                    more felt than seen.

Darlings

i.

"   your darlings."

These darlings
my darlings
I   nurtured them

Their
Sensitive

Their spirited

These darlings

so fresh with life

And open

You   made them
As much yours as any

                    the living
breathing
See
    darling   .

ii.

"Give us your darlings."

These darlings
          my darlings
I   nurtured them
Out of obscure language,
Their
Sensitive

Their spirited

These darlings cannot be
Contained,
          so fresh with life

  against the stillness
And open

You have made them now
As much yours as any

Frighteningly mythic
Images hewn into the living
Re-imagine their breathing

See
Their darling   .

iii.

"Give us your darlings."
—A call for Submissions

These darlings
Are no longer my darlings
I only nurtured them
Out of obscure language, stroked
Their soft heads and warm
Sensitive ears
Their slick fur, half shut eyes
Hearts that visibly beat
Through sharp ribs
As if to show their will
Their spirited
Guttural growl and snort
As they struggle and flop
These darlings cannot be
Contained, they wriggle and claw
So young, so fresh with life
Their tender paws and wings
Play against the stillness
And open themselves to
Misunderstanding, or
Creative misreading
You have made them now
As much yours as any
Bat, bird, or feral cat
Or gryphon-like, feral bat-cats
Prehistoric hieroglyph animals
Frighteningly mythic
Images hewn into the living
Re-imagine their breathing
Gently blow in their faces
See their needle-like teeth
Their darling teeth.

iv.

"Give us   ."
          —A Call For Submissions

Are no longer
  only
Out of obscure language, stroked
    soft heads and warm
          ears
    slick fur, half shut eyes
Hearts that visibly beat
Through sharp ribs
As if to show

Guttural growl and snort
      struggle and flop
          cannot be
Contained, they wriggle and claw
So young,
    tender paws and wings
Play
        themselves to
Misunderstanding, or
Creative misreading
      made   now

Bat, bird, or feral cat
Or gryphon-like, feral bat-cats
Prehistoric hieroglyph animals
Frighteningly mythic
Images
Re-imagine
Gently blow
        needle-like teeth
              teeth.

V.

"   ."
—A Call For Submissions

Are no longer
  only
                    language, stroked
      soft

      slick
            visibly

As if to show

      struggle

                  wriggle

Play

                  or
Creative misreading
            now

            mythic
Images
    -imagine

                  teeth
      teeth.

Overtime Reflects

Overtime like a mirror contemplatively reflects
on (while being in) the moment where self-aware
skin-flushed, naked, and lost

maybe something

something maybe

inherently blank
like a mirror Overtime contemplatively reflects.
Substantively immaterial, if not wholly conceptual.

Overtime and The Dance

Overtime no longer maintains control, the crowd
in its frenzy of immediacy and spontaneous
combustibility, excites the air   the walls   the space
between the air and walls, excites *thumpa-thumpa*
emerging rhythm, unaware that space now breathes
the bodies on their feet as they reach and reach.
Thumpa-thumpa, thumpa-thumpa. The heart translates
Overtime's singular thought underlying all thought
thumpa-thumpa: here, not-here; limited, delimited
over time, over what; and in the ecstasy of the eternal
present- Overtime *(unaware in the moment of itself)*
left the house; curling iron on, front door wide open
wandering among the masses gathered in the street
both of and beyond time- becomes self-forgetful.
Space no longer exists; everything holds together
from pure desire for harmony. Time and Overtime
reconcile, expanding the scope of whatever happens
in a perfected atmosphere. *Thumpa-thumpa*, the crowd
(like so many tenuous atoms held together then torn
apart and recombined by an unseen force) realigns
forming more stable structures, stronger relationships
thumpa-thumpa, the timeless beat pulses and thrums.
The crowd no longer maintains control over time.

Double Feature Westerns

Some movies are the same with different names.
I miss the double feature, miss A Fist Full
Of Dynamite and A Fist Full of Dollars
Spaghetti westerns with young Clint Eastwood
And Toco- the foolish, unconvincing, villain.
I still confuse Rio Bravo and El Dorado
Although Dean Martin is my favorite drunk
Vulnerable, uncertain, and inherently good
And John Wayne in every movie- even McQ
Is authentically *(if not expectedly)* the Duke.
After early dinner, the first show would go on
At Six and the second at Eight for fifty cents
Each, and I would see both even if the same
Spending hours on rainy days remembering
The details and differences between the stories
Who played who, what happened when
How mud on a boot leads to blood in a glass
Why good men live unspoken codes in the wild
Beyond a frontier where he that draws fastest
Shoots first, lives longest. Where new frontiers
Interpret morals of truth and justice into laws
Enforced by Sheriff and posse (civilized if
Black and white) and are judged in Technicolor
Determined sequel worthy- to ride again.
Sometimes a double feature is not enough.

Aliens and Zombies

Some movies I watch more than once.
Mostly comedies, dark comedies, horror movies-
Especially ones with aliens and zombies-
Fictions where, laughing, I surprise
Jo and the kids, and they nervously laugh along.
Then, days or weeks later, the same movie
Appears again, and I watch more intently
As hungry zombies trip all over themselves
Or aliens that look like us admire then
Conquer Earth quickly, but can't adapt.
New details emerge, and I find foreshadowing
In the face of the foreknown- like dying
Or not dying; or an afterlife, or this life.
I study these movies and suspend my disbelief
As if we could all be zombies or aliens, or both-
And conclude humanity is an everyday thing
Not just like on Sunday- where it is told
We are both of and not of this earth. How
In our fallen state we see ourselves better, then
Slowly trip all over ourselves wherever we go.

Overtime v. Later

Later lies, is a cheap impostor, Overtime
asserts coolly from the witness stand
under oath, a serious accusation, damning
and now lists the grievances, those failings
Later committed that Overtime suffers:
I will call you later; Pay you back next
week/month/year; I am busy, let's do it later
When you grow up you will understand
You can't know what is in The Bill until...
Tomorrow the delicious will taste even better
Save some for later; After this then that
(as if Later cannot manage multi-tasking).
The litany of abuses continues for Later
and Overtime mutters an outraged, *No!*
Later deceives, provides false promise
is a donkey in a lion suit, a hall of mirrors
a trap of expectations and unmet resolutions.
Later operates on credit; Overtime is gold.
Overtime embodies the spirit of possibility
to resolve the unresolved; once more finally
hope in redemptive beyond; absolution of Now.
Overtime facilitates, Later defers and excuses.
Overtime... is; Later lies a cheap impostor.

Overtime, The Moon, The End, and Us

When we sense the end is near, Overtime looms
in the near distance, like the harvest moon
close to the horizon, promising and large
in the dusky blue sky, the nightless moon.
And when we sense the night is over, too
when birds sing the sun into being, the moon
pales in a pale blue sky, and Overtime looms
again, like a reminder that nothing is over
day and night- night and day the large moon
varies in shadow and half-light, yet remains
as oceans know, the same. So, Overtime looms
before and after the moon: a shifting horizon
in an expanding universe of orbiting bodies
and round rocky worlds. Overtime looms
where things become new and where entropy
unravels, and we sense the end is near. We are
near the end, always near the end, the end
and Overtime looms, like the moon; the moon
although it too wanes is there, day and night
we sense when over time the end looms near, is
and Overtime is no longer. Then we all go home.

Savage Tendencies
for Colleen

I suggest you run. Three, two, one...
Then screaming ensues and paintballs
Like soft rocks, smack and splatter
So you find cover behind whatever
Locate your teammates, team-up
With friends, and get strategic.
This will take a while, the culling play
Even if a game, will be savage and
(After all what game isn't) based on life?
This is your reward for a week
At work camp in western Kentucky
Painting the home of an infirmed
Elderly woman who ran out of options.
"In the long run, *(pause)* we are all dead."
Says the economist and theorist
As he loads paintball bullets into
The machine of monetary policy
Which determines who lives and dies
Who produces (or not); who consumes.
This is your future we are speaking of...
Are you having fun? Have you learned?
Aim high, keep moving, shoot far, far
Cover fire is a good turn not forgotten.
Pace yourself, savagery can last lifetime.
Heed good advice when you hear it.

Cold Meatloaf Sandwich

A delicacy best savored standing
Over the kitchen sink looking out
Upwind from smoldering leaves
In November before turkey leftovers
Found two, maybe three days after
Covered at the back of the refrigerator
Before the tomato sauce has turned
With cracked pepper and mayonnaise
Reminding you of your mother's recipe
While the green pepper and onion effuse
Alone or when no one is watching
With a bottle of water, or ice water
Cold, cold, cold, cold and hungry
Like disappointment revisited.

Fogdune

Essential distance like forgetfulness
The necessary point-of-view for fog
From the coastal road, along the beach
A string of asphalt laid on ground shells
Or from the bluff above stepped tree tops
Fog billows-in subduing rough waters
Absorbing all that can't outrun
Or burrow beneath its granular grasp.
Here is the thing: Fog is disconcerting.
We see it coming, line of here and not
Then are in it not knowing its depths.
Down at the beach I wait, take a handful
Of sand, it streams through my fingers.
When the fog arrives, it will not be held
I breathe in the damp-cold, exhale fog.
I exhale fog, forgetting the damp-cold
Scribble in grains of fog my fading sense
Fogdune inside me, just beyond my grasp.

Sepia, Ink and Marble on Viscous Membrane

1.

Every tree in winter is a father's portrait.
Every wool coat, every knit hat and gloves
A mother's enduring love. We fade, and fade.
Every funeral parlor pin-board of memory
Has a half-dressed child standing implacably
Filthy from dust of their days, they smile
Their eyes are smiling with clenched fists
Determined to stay in that moment. *Click.*

2.

In those halcyon days of Caietae, Aeneas
At rest in the harbor of your childhood, Virgil
So named after your nurse, as you gazed out
Upon the spreading sea, divine mysteries
What is foretold and what remains unknown
Did you see the Kingfishers' nest afloat
In calm waters? Was it winter-smooth sea?
Is gravitas the wet mantle of remembered loss?

3.

Michelangelo's Pieta... look it up. Look.
Carrara marble, disproportionately large
Her draped body like a pyramid cradling
His extinguished self. Mother and child
Eternally alive in that cold moment.
Every sculpted rock is a little frozen death.
Our beautiful loss cries an ocean of tears.
Carry it inside you like ice until you float.

II.

Mid-Summer Daily

Exuberant vibration, unseen Cicada song
Drone of hot bees and honey bee throng

Combustion's cacophony on distant road
Campfire smoke from nearby campground

Cloudbanks disperse above sand dunes
Dusts slow convection in afternoon sun

Deciduous trees move in gentle breeze
The air is bathed in deep green leaves

Overripe bananas like banana bread
Warm punchy apples and peaches at rest

An extra-large envelope, open on my desk
My lungs fill with poems daily like this.

Ambersong

1.

I sing of towering ancient pines
                    and resin
and Nature's resonance within our cavities
our head, and throat, and chest:
Visceral, slow,
                    qualitative and comparable.
Is it such a leap
                    to find commonality
among the swaying pines?
Is it any less ambitious discovering the ways
of wooded passages
                    and monuments they build?
How similar it all becomes-
                    trunks, limbs, bark-
once inside the forest. The path that deer tread
leads to byways of coyotes and bears,
                    and men
in search of certain ways across the rock
and needle strewn forest floor;
                    darkened pine
maze and mossy tree tunnel that silently shield
our pilgrimage,
                    filter the sun and moonlight glow
that permeate this directionless woods,
                    where
we lose each other and ourselves. If you must
look up,
          the lowest branches bristle at the sun.

2.

Small pockets of Neolithic air,
                          a cloudy vein
of tiny bubbles like rain, fine mist
                          in amber beads-
mist of time before steel, before stone tools-
pre-fog of history, fog of then-
                          hold your breath
   start counting to ten-million:

                          Now let it out
all of it and more. The last of it is lung fog-
little unspokenness
                    of life, withheld words; mist
of first loves, unconditional mist
                          given, forgiven-
grainy truths. Perceptive pockets form everywhere
and cloud once soft blobs of resin
                          as if trees mourn
or bleed amber under the stress of time,
                          or exhale
fossilized air; small love, small truth-
                          breathe deep.
What is ten million years
                    if not fine mist in amber?

3.

In the forest of the mind, all trees are otherness.
Each original, each earth-bound; invisibly
breeze swept, confused
                         tufted heads nod in waves.
Call it madness, weird, or how awareness would be
if we were trees.
                         Their root systems interwoven
like mother-child, brothers and sisters, memory
of famine, memory of flood;
                         needle strewn floor
needle filled sky, what happened and will happen
trees know-
               and somehow, my friend, so do you.
You know the tongue of towering pines and feel
the implacable whisper of trees.
                         Are you listening?
The trees keep speaking, walk among them now
in gentlest wind they whisper,
                         in softest rain
they murmur the unspoken
                         vanity of half truths
they see themselves in us walking among them
brothers and sisters, mirrored
                         in silver rivers
gently flowing past-
                         think they can walk memory
through their roots,
                         in amber beads measure time
with just one ring each year-
                         residue of unspent
resins, this year's scar for willfully deluded pines
in the forest of the mind,
                         all trees are otherness.

4.

The deep blue wonder
        of Dominican amber.
The oldest equatorial evergreen island amber
mined between
        Caribbean blue sky and sea
the same tropical species of conifer found
in Africa and India.
        Place the stone on a field
of white and shine light upon it
        and through it
yellow shades yawn and wave.
        Now on a field
of darkness, of that buried beneath mountains
or cast farthest away from the sun
        and watch-
the amber turns blue, without a refracting field
the stone of itself alters wavelength, iridescent
if not radiant, with only the faintest yellow hint
and residues of rusty hues,
        earthly impurities
caught in amber; flecks of tree matter, dirt
gnats, wasps, roaches-
        mosquitoes in movies
where dinosaur DNA is reclaimed, cloned
for our entertainment-
        an engineered clarity
where the organic beyond our comprehension
cannot satisfy our senses.
        I see through amber
if not beyond, and wonder
        whose idea was this
that this blue world is our domain in a Universe
with translucent rules
        designed by what or who?

5.

In the forest of the body,
                        two snakes entwine
beneath the pine needles and spent cones, their
double helix of desire, each writhing for the other
has them mimic all life
                        at the cellular level- as
Celtic knots do the atomic.
                        Yet I digress from The Act
where Tiresias stumbled upon the copulating snakes
and for reasons still unclear today,
                        beat them
in the midst of procreation... His first mistake
in a Universe that favors life,
                        which fathered
a series of misadventures until Tiresias retired.
And in retirement, hiking
                        among the Greek hills
beneath the *Pinus Nigra* (Black Pine), the gods
who in life alternately made him
                        man and woman
blind and all-seeing, interpreter of bird songs
and omens, of this and the other world
                        finally
released Tiresias of his body, then transformed
him into dirt
                        and whatever else of Tiresias endures
n Asphodel meadows, while here pine cones spiral
n a Fibonacci dance of life-
                        a Celtic interlace band
or meandering pattern key, life beginning as it ends
male and female;
                        scales of seed, scales of pollen
then a double helix, some of this and some of that
two snakes entwined
                        in the forest of the body.

6.

"*The Soul selects her own Society*"
                              -Emily Dickenson

Norwegian star touched pines
                    in stands of three
their slender trunks like tall ship masts.
Softer red and common white pines, two by two
along the lakeshore
                    rooted in sandy loam.
Pre-historic Lebanese and Baltic pines,
                                   divine
conifers subjected to the weight of time-
cycles and events.
                    Interconnectedness of root
society of thermodynamics, sequence of sun
and rain, the slow turn
                    of growth; needle drop
on the matted forest floor, soft if not selective.
Whatever soulfulness
                    Creation imparts here
whatever endures immutably in our Nature
the brilliance of stars, invisible genius of Law
manifests in society; the felicity
                    of evergreens
with their narrow, petal-like
                    mirrored leaves.
Their resins in veins bleed, harden imperfectly
a hardness *like stone-*
                    organic as my amber song
this breath I share,
                    this star touched Soul I squeeze.

7.

The forest spirits rest in the highest boughs
of conifers- quiet
          then morning songs of birds
squirrel chatter, buzz of fly warmed by the sun
in perfumed pine boughs. The highest branches
sway and bounce in the breeze unfelt below
along the darkened forest floor-
            musty, fetid
fit for mushrooms and moss, where abandoned
and broken boughs-
          rigid as pegs or ladder rungs
their needle and cone days forever past, remind
of Nature's imperative to rise or else.
At night
         spirits move in moon shadows, protecting all
held together by skin of light
             against annihilation.
Injured and healing pines, releasing amber resin
lean on the upright,
          rub their song like horsehair
across strung catgut; *here, here, here, here, here*
vibrates off their spruce soundboard.
              Music elevates
in widening circles from seedling to piney tip top.
This is the forest's ceremony for the dying trees.
Their only word groaned-out one last time, nearly
indecipherable in the wind-
         their empty anguish
sways and creaks its requiem in "D", composing
their last note while decomposing.
             Each movement
furthers, each remembers- an amber elegy, this
hardening song
        that softly plays like forest spirits.

8.

Late winter thaw-
          the snow packed trail alternates
from heavy wet to shady ice,
                    and unfolds unseen
the brutal seasons that melt
                    and fade to nothingness.
Today the snowpack glare, stark and overwhelming
compels my eyes to seek shade
                    in a thick of pines.
Here the snow, ice crusted from the occasional light
balances needles
          among oversized tracks- distilled
snow, an opposition to the amber ways of whiskey
where impurities are removed
                    instead exposes a slurry
of tree bark, rabbit scat, pine cone petals, and twigs
the crusted sleep around Nature's eyes and mouth
as if Nature sleeps like we sleep, which it doesn't
although
          our *animus* shares an affinity for the wild
unbridled, nose in the wind, bared teeth and claw
ways of Nature,
          who isn't ecstatic to pass beyond
and into the wonder of that palpable difference
which transcends;
                    our resonant and enduring song?
So, when my eyes narrow and burn from blinding
glare- and truth distorts for lack of contrast-
                                        I'll seek
my solace and comfort, not in the shade of stands
but in highest perfumed boughs
                    of sun strewn pine
where I will sing my Ambersong to earth and sky.

October's Cricket

I hear you, October's cricket
On this warm afternoon, out by
The walking path
Your *chirp-chirp-chirp*
Drones past at the speed of my gate
And I can't stop for fear
If I did then you would
And we wouldn't want that
Wouldn't want to stop being
In this mild October moment
Where I long to be
And for perhaps the first time
Hear you clearly, picture you alone
Among the straw grasses
By the gravel shoulder singing out
Your inexhaustible song
For perhaps the very last time
Just for me as I pass.
I will sing that song all winter long.

Return of the Sparrows

Too many strands of lights
For me alone to unravel and display
In just one day
Before Christmas, so I resolved
To start the first Sunday of Advent
With the Poplar
At the front corner of our house
And each Sunday throughout the season
String more lights
Through the Holly bushes beneath
Colleen's bedroom window
Then wrap the one porch pillar
Up and across the archway
Then down the other pillar, until at last
On the final weekend Joanne and I
Wrap the trunk and limbs
Of our Japanese Maple in front
Of my office windows.
I did not write much in December
As our lights stay lit
For the twelve days of Christmas
That follow into the New Year.
Even after twelve days
The three wise men lingered
In silence after Mass-
The nativity scene and crèche
Remaining in the gathering space
A reminder perhaps that the wise men
Are simply travelers from the East.
So I put our Christmas lights away.
Today the sparrows excitedly returned.
Their hunger pecks and flits.

Lakeshore Rafter Migration

They keep emerging from the woods.
I might see them once a year
Headed west toward the lake
For no reason, as no one has ever
Seen them swim
(Not even the Discovery Channel)
Yet, with little over a rolling mile
Of summer homes and cottages remaining
To the shore of Lake Michigan
Turkeys confidently stream out
Onto my front yard
Under this overcast September sky
And steadily advance across my driveway
And into my neighbors yard
With purpose toward the unseen lake.
The entire gang ambles along
(As if convicted or compelled
By forces beyond their understanding)
Disregarding all the facts
That there is no grand suspension bridge
No bay for mooring or wharf
No tall ship waiting for them to depart.
So *what then* when they get there?
If they can swim like penguins
Or flock like wild geese
Or utter invocations and offerings
And make the waters part like Moses
They could possibly end up in Milwaukee.
I'm grabbing sandals, going to the beach.

Sunset at the Beach, Late July

1.

The waves murmur, appear distraught
Concerned about
                 I don't know, their lips
Flap in the breeze, meaning is lost or hidden
Like schools of Rainbow Trout rippling
                 for evening shadows;
For calm, reflective moments where at dusk
Flies skitter and rest quietly in shallows.
If only I could translate
                 their wavy consternations.

2.

Curious how the waves here stop then
                 the tree line also stops
Along the lakeshore. Haltingly I wade
                 into their pooling thoughts;
Tentatively, stare back from the shallows
Gaze at the narrow horizon of last light
                 the rolling waves and sand
                 dunes along the tree line
First stars that twinkle, red planets at dusk
                 low along the horizon.
There are more stars than grains of sand
The waves observe. Here there is no alone
                 listen, listen,   listen.

3.

There are monarch butterflies migrating.
There are grasshoppers and beetles;
                    they cling to tall dune grasses.
There is visible wind invisibly migrating;
                    among transforming clouds
                    within foaming white caps
                    through bending dune grasses
                    under the wings of gulls
                    across drifting sands
                    into and out of leaves and lungs.
There is sunlight waning and moonlight
                    whispering small truths.
The giant ear of everything here listens
                    closely like a wakeful parent.
There is my shadow stretching across the sand
The drifting gull hovers, dives into relevance;
                    we all sense our purpose here.

4.

Saplings line the low bluff beyond the reach
                    of tidewaters and sand.
They loosely hold their ground, birch and pine
                    slow to move or judge
                    discerning with gentle nods.
I vaguely sense their unspoken concerns as well
                    and share my trepidation.
The tide rolls, the sands shift, the sun returneth.
Every tree casts shade, beyond the line is shade.
                    Sunset is a thin proposition.

5.

The many prints of travelers fade into the sand;
                   at last- gull, wave, beetle, poet
Shadows are all now although
                  even shadows softly speak.

Forecasts

The air is unstable and builds clouds
Inland as weather moves off the big lake
This evening like so many other summer
Evenings when a front comes through
And storms break loose. The hummingbird
Is back at seventy beats per second, wings
A blur of shade around its' suspended body
Iridescent, small, steady and quick.
It sees the ultraviolet, hears distant thunder.
Today there is a heat advisory, the app
On my Galaxy 5 forecasts storms tonight
Ninety-two with eighty percent humidity
The hummingbird must like that being
One hundred and seven itself and nearly
Ten percent brain and heart. Extraordinary.
It remembers the flowers in our garden.
It will shake my bed as I try to fall asleep.

North Texas Rain

for Cousin Angela

Hard rain for days, thick as bees
Flooding nightly on the national news
All spring; beds swollen beyond full
Roads washed out, forty plus head
At Red River Breaks gone missing
And now your twin sister, Virginia
After her long battle has gone beyond
Our grasp, beyond plain and hillcrest.
It used to be weddings and birthdays
Now I only ever see you at funerals
So when you call days before her
Memorial service to verify the dates
Of our grandparents deaths, long ago
And you need to get off the phone
As it is raining again, the steady drone
On your roof and windows is calling
You hold me in silence for a breath
And I hear the rain in north Texas.

Inspired by an Elegy

I strike a match against my shoe.
It is something I saw in a movie
Or read in a book, or heard in a song
You scrape a wooden match stick
(Paper is too flimsy, it must be wood)
So quick, the friction you generate
Forcing the tip across a rough surface
The scuffed bottom of your shoe or heel
The rubbing heat excites the sulphur
Which first begins to glow, then flashes
And, *Whoosh...* the tip sparks into flame
And settles into a slow, even burn
(When you hold the stick just right)
Which is all I need to light this life
Like a prayer candle or big cigar
To push-back against the nothingness
With ambient glow, or halo of light
Or expanding puff of near-white smoke.
Anyhow, it wasn't my idea... *fire.*
Still, in my funeral suit and best shoes
I travel now with a box of matches.

Late Winter Ice Storm

Empty roads slide past
February's frozen buds
Rabbits in their den.

Birds in March

I can't tell you what you
Do not know, birds in March
Outside perched on leafless
Limbs. I'm a prisoner
Bound by conventions, these
Glasses, these sun glasses
My watch and silver chain
My cotton underwear
(We grow no cotton here)
Although our house is warm.
Your innocent wisdom
Staring through my office
Window, makes me shiver
Or is it your regret
That you are not inside
That gardens grow outside
Or how the trees are bare?

El Nino

Little one
Thin with snows
Little Winter
Lamb of Winter
No wind, no chime
Not yet February
The sun extends
Patches of blue sky
The poplar buds
Little fur folds
The same sun
Gently extends
Patches of grass
Brown grass.

Ode to a Recycling Bin

Earth saver
Bin of our redemption
On street or back alley.
Imaginations' ally
Remaker of the spent
You never touch
The same used thing
The same way twice.
Bin of possibilities
Bin of tomorrows headlines
Newspaper or toilet paper
What was and will be.
Bin of conscience balm.
Ecclesiastic
Plastic to plastic
And dust to dust
Bin of *returneth again.*
For bottles without deposits.
For paper that will not burn
Corrugated boxes and catalogues.
Bin of the online shopper's
Packing bubble sheets.
For the tin in your can
The lid from your jam.
Oh, Recycling Bin!
You are trash's good twin.
That I could crawl
Inside you and dream.

Complicity

The trees dance
 In spring air
And sunlight
Soft sunlight
Thin vertical
Poplar branches nearly
Vibrate, and pine
Boughs bob
I observe
Withhold judgment.
Still the wind chime
Outside
My window is
Mute this morning
Tongue in cheek
Sends me
A knowing look.
Alright
We're good here.

Au Sable at Dawn

Here, being first on the river matters.
Before the dawn stars give way
To planets then blue sky, the river
Forgets the past like a mirror
And promises to picnic with you
When the sun is too high and hot
And your neck and arms grow weary
(As far as promises go, that's not bad
A guide and traveling companion
That shows sweetly and provides).
Our paddles are the first disturbance
But there is no echo on the river
Only a dusting of pre-dawn mist
That dips and swirls, and rises is lost
Like our whispers that dissipate
And soon, beavers scramble in shallows
Trout rise and feed on floating circles
The first heron unsettles and swoops.
So we travel between shadowed banks
Chasing a liquid rail of what is
That moves us ever further downstream
Understanding why being first matters
And how unfamiliar we are on the river.

III.

On Leaving Little Traverse

Boxes and boxes of books, broken frames
June's poinsettia, shoes,
                  this week's
Laundry heaped in an open basket

The bay immense like God's ear
An open bowl
             that spills resplendent sunsets.

Grey lake, beach then dune,
                   ski hills
And hills, grey rain, an elevated horizon
Without snow,
            grey clouds without sky-
Grinding in low gear, all the harder
Headed up-hill,
            beyond the ridge
And the next, the next, if necessary
All the way home,
            back home again-
An echo of cloud the answer to my prayer.

The Warriors

After the fighting ends
The Warriors
Their farms and families tended
Their well source secure
Begin to stack rock and build
Stables, granaries, a mill on the river
In whatever jurisdiction they hold
And pay tribute for. Then,
exhausted
Take refuge in memory, prepare for war
By reading books and sharpening swords
Their oppressors have dulled
Through peace and litigation.
They state dissatisfaction
With the undoing they endure
In crafted letters, essays, and poems
As they scratch out their landscape
In furrowed lines and shifting horizons
With fragile nibs pinched
Tenuously between
Their bloodied fingers.
If they survive the undoing
Their next battle will be glorious.

Servings

Everything gets measured before cooking
Not after the grease
Has been sweated-out
Or spinach and berries wilt-off their
Nutrients and water weight. None of this
Mattered until
My health app updated
And my obsession with
Walking the dogs
Ten thousand steps a day, now
That I'm over Fifty, became a real measure
(Moment by moment in varying lines)
Of health and fitness.
Wondering why I am
What I am, I document
My meals *(and snacks, although*
I didn't know there were Snack tabs
Until late yesterday) recording each item
And number of servings
Then seeing calories, and ratios
Of nutrients, carbohydrates, fats
And assorted vitamins.
The bad news is
The app also charts my sleep.
The good news is one serving
Of Irish whiskey
Contains only sixty-nine calories
So I portion three when
I pour myself one
While preparing dinner
(Which sounds like a whiskey
Fueled exaggeration, or
A thoughtless ritual) as I am uncertain
Just what constitutes a Serving.

The Emergent Poet at Fifty

Some things I never tire of
Like reflections of the moon
(The big early moon seen through trees)
On water or any large window.
Apple fritters and cigars for breakfast
And a few hours, or eighteen
Dew wetted holes, to burn at play.
Good poetry-
Not great, just well-crafted and smacking
Of truth.
Acres of husky stalks of corn, chest-high
In windswept fields where clouds of
Birds dive and whirl, then settle
Beneath the golden waves.
Matinee Tigers' baseball in May
Or late September, but not midsummer.
Frothy whitecaps as the day heats
And gusts relentlessly from the west
Over the big lake.
Barbeque anything
Especially grilled salmon and asparagus
With Caesar salad and Pinot Noir.
Bats at dusk feeding on invisibly small
And illusive mosquitoes, swollen
From their last meal.
Nearly uncontrollable bonfires
Surrounded by
Marshmallows ready to also burst.
Friends that harmlessly flirt
And are unabashedly good at it.
Wink, wink.

Waking up pre-dawn with the dull ache
Of yesterday's landscape labors
And needing to go, then climbing back
Into the warm bed, drowsy
Vaguely satisfied, and stiff.
These days and nights, and things
That play with light.
Is this so wrong to admit?

Wink.

Excavations

i.m. Seamus Heaney(1939-2013)

Typically it is infrastructure
Being built
New foundations being dug
Trenching to lay pipe or cable
Or piers and footings for skyscrapers
The Shard, Khalifa, One World Trade
Some massive undertaking
Where entire cities are re-engineered
And disrupted
By unearthed discoveries
Ruins, time capsules, bones
And we reflect as time wavers
In layers of sediment
Our lives spent, our sentiment
And history revisions us.
Then again occasionally
In remote desert areas
A hidden chamber is revealed
By archeologists dressed in linen
Beneath a temple or tomb
Fragments with chiseled figures emerge
Under the oppressive
Heat and ancient sands are brushed aside
From mysterious granite slabs
By clean fingers
Delighted and awed, and self-effacing
At their new found smallness.
Or more recently, local seekers
In the Channel Islands
Following lore sung in public houses
Or rhymes taught in school
And using detectors
Exposed a long lost trove

Of Roman and Celtic coins
Obscured by hedge rows
Their silver glint diminished
By the darkness
Sealed inside of earthen jars.
In any case, I am reminded that
Even if largely buried
Or reclaimed by the elements
Our history is a history
Of cuneiforms and hieroglyphs
Animal heads on human bodies
Or rough hewn animal bodies
Silently standing sentinel
And crudely stamped human heads
Issued by governments on silver
Another reminder
Like hedge rows or trenches
Of men that claimed supremacy
In the name of civilization
Over other men
Whose names are reduced by the sands
Or worn away by rain and wind
And forgotten
Or erased from ledgers, or changed
Like so many rebel patriots, emigrants
Into a new world of strange landscapes
That were and now are
Gone astray-
Their names no longer referenced
Their sound lost is our lost sound
And it becomes personal, here
The tongue has been granted the right
To reclaim the past unspoken

Our long silence broken
Around the dinner table at holiday
Between family-
Who we are no longer
Where we came from no more
Any last treasures worth exposing
Monuments to the present sharing
Lines cut in granite. So
Walk on air... it is
Against your better judgment- Spirited.
Under the Christmas lights- with Larkin
Unfazed- in Tollund
Animated- *your stick in the air.*
Like... *Moths then on evening water*
Incorruptible by darkness
It would have to be, not butterflies in sunlight-
Against the rain and whispering sands
Expressing all
We lived and loved, our lost and found.

Overtime and Charley

Overtime lives with my father in Florida.
He said, *I didn't expect to still be here*
in umbrella strewn shade of his poolside
lawn chair, his face lifts and incidental scars
measure the distance between us, and now
like abandoned frontier outposts, eerily they
remind of better days, the glory days.
After The War he served in the occupation
while shit got sorted-out, and teenage
Somethings ran amok within the ranks
going nowhere, which is when Overtime-
sensing the zero sum game some men play
in life and death (their lives and deaths)-
stowed away in his duffle as a souvenir
of war, and demobilized with my father.
Charley played basketball on the G.I. Bill
and Overtime cheered wildly, as he studied
Commerce and Finance at university.
Sensing, later at dark hours when the bars
were closed and birds slept, that somehow
he possessed otherworldly greatness (as if
Overtime conveyed the powers of Krypton)
he would teach me about codependency and
Overtime, while sipping Old Fashioneds.
My father in Florida lives with Overtime.
He said, *I didn't expect to still be here.*
So, we watch college basketball and cheer.

Overtime Gets Real

When the sun sets and rises and returns, Overtime
turns up, punches in, logs on, and smiles at us
sunglasses in pocket- useful at dusk and dawn-
and a brimless indoor/outdoor hat- for style-
joyfully humming overtures and requiems
and is requested over the loud speakers
to report to the front office; time for Overtime
amidst the cheers and groans, intoxicated
Amens and shouts of Hallelujah Lord
our side bets and over-unders still in play
to run their undulating uncharted course-
abundantly pleased as our expectations
for an unmet end are surprisingly met
when the sun sets and rises and over time returns.
Dutifully, Overtime begins where vanity ends.

Overtime and Golf

There is no Overtime in the Devil's Game, Golf
only rules to be broken, argued, or kept sacred
the social conventions of civilized games
with no exceptions for exemptions in Spring
when wet fairways plug, or leaf strewn late Fall
when I've often lost a ball and taken my penalty
for long shots misplayed in deep rough and heather.
What would you do here? I would go for the green.
We never tell the story about how we didn't
(note: stories about golf are different than Overtime)
on a Sunday morning, church-bells in the distance
put back the three iron and grip our self-indulgent
ill-advised driver; humbly swung and sweetly met.
A game of loving your neighbor as yourself: Golf.
No *two off the tee* Mulligan's. No *roll 'em in
the fairway.* No *animal hole must have got it
drop and play.* No *stealing the tee box, hit up
when ready, practice in the hazard.* No *do-overs.*
Rules to be broken, argued, or kept sacred. Only
in golf (the Devil's Game) is there no Overtime.

Ode to a Tee Box

I must bring all the club, spare ball and tees
That I may need
And confidently approach you
By cart from the winding path
Or carrying my bag on foot from the last green
Or by the wayward meandering
And luxurious freedom of hand cart
And grasp all the clubs deemed
Vital and necessary and true
For the fulfillment
Of my strategic approach to distant green.
You are elevated and tight and square
My imagined parallelogram
Two club lengths behind the markers
And up as nature allows
Carved from and into the wilderness.
Oh, Tee Box!
You shape the course.
You align the stars in heaven.
You are my standing ground.
Singularly you expand consciousness
From here I reach beyond the horizon
Across rooftops and church steeples
I grasp at ethers and clouds.
From your table my eyes feast
Upon this landscape of desire
A perilous future of small windows
Waste bunkers, heather, rolling fairways.
That I could stay indefinitely
Within the frame of your timeless embrace
And contemplate the tallest pine in spring
The yellow birch nestled in fall
The cry of marsh-hawk beyond the crest
And chatter of tree-line squirrels
As siren-like they vie for my intention.

Oh Tee Box!
You humble me to the one thought
A confluence of breath
The movement of swing
And a last vision of what can be.
The deep regret I have
At withdrawing to reconsider
My dubious club selection
The lost sense of purpose and conviction
At stepping back from your narrow promise.
(No soul should ever suffer an eternity
Chasing ghosts, hazardous shots repeated
When facing your certainty unprepared.)
Oh, Tee Box! You are Charon's skiff
The deck from which all souls
Resign and gird themselves then depart.
Here I seek another world to discover
That which escapes me; the illusive harmony
The genius of your perspective
Met with my passionately released swing.
I gladly sacrifice my body
My feet firmly planted in your sod
My head still, unwavering as a hummingbird's
While madly beating wings invisibly
Lift my spirit, try my strength and will.

Ode to Interview Questions

Tell me about yourself, let's warm up
How did you dress at your last job?
How would your co-workers describe you?
Or share some lies about your passion
For canned green beans and rice
For Our Lord and Savior Jesus Christ
For your neighbor's leaky roof
Are you warm yet, let's try the truth?
How do you feel about Depoprovera
For a mother of two that cries *No mas*
A donation only Laundromat or Viagra
For the transient homeless on parole?
What would you do to promote
Mission, expand program outreach
Encourage volunteerism, generate
Major gift increases of twenty percent?
(s it me or is it *really* warm in here?)
Can you tell us a joke?
What is your greatest strength/weakness?
Do you know Tommy Betrus?
Why did you attend the University
Of Michigan to study Liberal Arts?
What brought you to west Michigan?
Are you good at telling stories?
Business casual, in Petoskey only
Salesmen wear a tie. Yes, the truth.
Prescriptions without performance
Are often more addictive than outcomes.
Yes. I am resilient with a sense of humor.
I can transcend time where all life becomes
Beautifully luminous- so willful madness
In the name of the creative act which is both
Would be my strength and weakness.
(I think it's really me that's warm in here.)
Did you hear the DNR created a hybrid

Sport-fish called a Co-Wall-Ske? Now
They just have to teach it how to swim.
(That's a Co-ho, a Walleye, and a Muske.)
They offered unparalleled programs.
Love, Faith in Providence, and a U-Haul.
Of course, who doesn't know Tommy B?
(Is every candidate asked these questions?)
Oh, interview questions you expose so much
I don't know. *What color would you be
If you were... or if you were simply me?*

Salty Days

For Dr. Adam Fogg

Doc Fogg says I shouldn't eat
Potatoes, Pasta, Bread, Sugar
¬hat my body craves salt, sea salt
¬hat I should take supplements
For my heart, cholesterol, liver:
Niacin, Red Yeast Rice, Milk
¬histle. *Listen*, I say how about
Cheeseburgers, hold the fries
Substitute a side of green beans
Or how about a side of pretzels
And mustard (with extra sea salt):
Salmon with (no potatoes) brown rice:
Harvest salad, dressing on the side
With grilled chicken, not fried:
Or the Ploughman's lunch
(lean meats, cheeses, boiled eggs
And raw seasonal vegetables)?
That, says Doc Fogg, sounds delicious
But, take a tablespoon of Apple
Cider Vinegar with the Mother first
And he'll see me again next month.
Sounds better than me going under
The knife, cutting these days short
My salty flesh
            and bone numbered days.

More Whiskey Please

Irish whiskey, bourbon whiskey
Eighteen year scotch,
                    my brain runs hot
This Friday night, around my hearth
Behind locked doors, there opens
                              questions
You shouldn't ask. I'm drunk for sure
And tell no lies; we've been married
Too long to quibble terms.
                    So don't ask
If I would come into the office now
Defrag and clean your hard drive. Don't ask
If I would step into the kitchen next
And load the empty dishwasher. Don't ask
If I would paint our country home
A shade of plum or peach. Don't ask
If I would lift your dowry chest again
Up the narrow stair and through
The archway by your bedroom
And gently rest it there. Don't ask
If I would start a war for your
Most friendly thighs and blousy lips
Matching kingdom for kingdom- acres
And chattel, friends and gifts.
                    Don't ask.
We've been married too long, and I
Am still in love with the dishwasher
Your colors, archways, our friendly fights
These whiskey Friday nights.
                    I might just sigh
Under the weight of your crooked smile
And say, *Yes, my love,*
                    more whiskey, please.

Lent Begins a Week Early

Fat Tuesday before Fat Tuesday.

Your father is in the hospital, he fell
Ever so slowly; ten short steps
From curb to door
                    ten steps.

She's trying to kill me, he says.
She says, *He won't let them operate.*

The next flight is Wednesday a.m.

The bottle is empty, Jo gets another.
Tomorrow may last forever.

Thirtieth October Sky

For Joanne

I read the sky
She lets me read her.
It will be cold
I say; yes, she says.
She knows I know the sky
Still she is not happy.
She is cold. She says
The sky is so blue today.
Yes, yes
It is, I say, and grey
so very grey
later today.
We are getting old
which is happy.
This is our happiness.
I tell her
Yes, yes.
It is how we
embrace the cold.

Overtime and The Hours

When there remains only hours, Overtime
begins speaking with authority, at first repeating
our favorite words and phrases, ones with praises
ones our parents would say relaxing late at night
ones familiar by day- *more iced tea, thank you*
where's your sister? I don't want this *or* that.
Minute, insecure, self-absorbed and essential.
Then as the hours progress and our failings are
exposed (pulse seventy-seven; RR nineteen; SpO2
ninety-one; BP one twenty-three over forty-two
hope in a higher power- rising; resolve- falling)
Overtime takes advantage of our frail condition
suggesting I get the car and we go home now
with almost angelic fervor, the music of delight
and look of wonder at the best idea ever- *let's go.*
The tubes beg to differ and monitors disagree.
The wall reminds us how late it has become and
the window agrees; it is late. Of course, the problem
of pain cannot be ignored for long, it will rain.
I did not bring the car that outruns inevitability
its' belts are being serviced, fluids refreshed
and then I want it detailed for our trip, I tell
Overtime, when there remains only hours.
After the hours have passed, I will bring you home.

Snow Drift

i.m. Charles W. Jones (1926-2016)

Tonight drifts of powdery snow obscure
The corners of your intransigent heart
The gratuitous head shot with tuxedo

Where the path is and where it leads
Ice covered pavement by the downspout
What we thought we knew about you

The resume you would never need
Chocolate sauce on Vanilla ice cream
Casablanca Lily's and your florist

Interior design v. development project
Your steadfast affections and illicit loves
Ice where sun shone, ice on headstone

Cold of space at night with moon glare
How it began here and ended over there
How memory's crust hardens over time.

The Surviving

Born in Detroit
the man was both
a commanding pres-
ence and
an object
lesson in tenacity.
Son of
the deceased.
Resident of
Palm Coast
Formerly Pres-
ident of
‾aylor Machine
Products, Inc.
What worked
for him
worked
for him.
Surviving are
his sister
his wife
his first wife
their three
adopted children
and eleven
grandchildren
many who love
'Westerns
golf and ice-cream
also.

Dark Star Sapphire

I am not sure what you thought of him those many days
My dark star sapphire set in fourteen karat gold
You are one of a few mementos he passed along
After he passed along leaving us here alone.
Can you read lips? Do you know how to sing?
Have you written a poem before or is this your first?
Have you seen the sun rise on your way home?
Have you been to an Irish pub for a pint?
Sparkled at the well timed telling of a racy joke?
Have you shopped beneath fluorescent lights
(In search of liquid aspirin, diapers, wipes) at 4 a.m.?
When was the last time you had a cigar my friend?
Last Sunday as you begged off sunrise service
You missed reading from the Book of the Prophet
Isaiah.
You should hear the fears and suffering of teenage girls.
This could be the beginning of a beautiful friendship.
Let's watch *Casablanca* with Humphrey Bogart.
Let's go to Canada and smuggle back duty free whiskey.
It's time for us to drive one-hundred-fifty in a seventy-
five miles-per-hour zone
In my 928S4 (its engine can power a small plane).
It's time we Zipline down the side of a mountain
Our feet dangling above the canopy, then into the trees.
It's time we built a bonfire of natural profit too big
Risking both incineration and incarceration at once.
It's time we hiked the Riley Trails, sweating
The cries of coyotes echoing downwind.
Next month we will do a reading and book signing.
It's time we share this brief life worth living.
It's time we established a correlative of our own.

March Again, Another Birthday

March thaws, the ground gives up
Its ghosts in pools of wet, pools of grey
Unsustainable seasonal greens then
March freezes again, scattering more
White, fresh on its unshaven face
Until the sun arrives, if it ever does.
You have been on my mind daily
This month, March. You reach out
From beneath our feet, reflecting feet
You coalesce in crystal whiteness
Out of pre-dawn air, shade of mist
On leaves of grass, on roof shingles
On my chin and cheeks in widening
Patches the sun can never fully thaw.
This March is a frosted carrot cake
Donut, enjoyed best with black coffee.

Overtime and Endings

Endings are not the end Overtime implies
as it leans over casually, confidently, drink
resting at its elbow- ice melted into small
white flakes of whatever residue resides
inside of freezer ice trays or water lines
(carbonates, chlorides, calcium, memories)-
its booziness thinned with eventualities
the added water and mineral deposits of ice
going the way of all things material. Overtime
begins to clear its' throat as if to say, *Not
so fast now* or simply to shift attention from
the was and what is to the what will be until
and drinks to all time; calcium and memory
(here is the bone, remember the bodily life).
Still, Overtime causally implies endings
and continuity; something else remains
in the rocks glass as the days' ending nears
a palpable change- an unfinished disillusion
of spirits, undissolved flecks in melted ice-
stories of transformation, what begins anew
and what endures after the moment melts.
Overtime implies endings are not the End.

Author's Notes

"Ausonius at Moselle" The Moselle is a river in Burgandy, France, which bordered Ausonius' estate where he fled in exile late in life. Translation is from the opening of his pastoral; Mosella Edyll III, 1-4:

Transieram clelrem nebulouso flumine Nauam,
Addita miratus veterinoua moenia vico;
Aequavit Latias ubi quondam Gallia Cannas
Inflletaeque iacent inopes super arua cateruce.

"Round Trip" and "Ode to a Massage Chair" were written following a trip to visit (care for) my father in Florida while his wife visited family in NYC for a week. It was a terrible trip down that involved several delays and re-routing. And, I humorously dreaded the travel back, which took me much farther North than seemed reasonable (Minneapolis? Why not Chicago, it's closer?). Yet, after the arduous experience of travel and caring for my father, I was simply left with an overwhelming sense of gratitude, gratitude for time well spent; and the largesse of grace, perhaps. So there were two poems, the poem of odyssey ("Round Trip") and the poem of gratitude (the Ode, in praise of a massage chair).

"Holland Lakeshore Fogbank" revisions Chicago poet Carl Sandburg's poem "Fog" from across the big lake, decades later, where it has moved on. *THE fog comes/ on little cat feet.// It sits looking/ over harbor and city/ on silent haunches/ and then moves on.*

"Darlings" was another poem which started as one thing (a rant upon reading a call for submissions from a literary journal which had recently rejected my poetry) and revealed another (a poem about poetry). However, upon Deconstructing the poem there became apparent a confluence of two subjects; poem as tender animal and poem as fierce language. Often Deconstruction can serve as a form of negation, here it revealed the opposite- multiple states.

"Savage Tendencies" *I suggest you run...* is the advice a parent-chaperone gave my daughter Colleen on her high school mission trip while playing paintball (a survival game where players hunt each other) their final day. She ran, and hunted. *"In the long run we are all dead."* –John Maynard Keynes (1883-1946), Economist known for promoting government deficit spending.

"Ambersong; 5" re-visions the death of Tiresias (the seer) near Mount Telphosion. Here Tiresias' body decays (is transformed) into dirt while his spirit endures intact in Asphodel meadows, a final gift from the Gods.

"Ambersong; 6" in considering soulfulness (following sections 3 and 5, mind and body) references Emily Dickinson's poem: *The Soul selects her own Society-/*

"Excavations" employs John Dryden's prefatory analogy of poet as builder (*Fables, Ancient and Modern*, 1713), while incorporating Seamus Heaney's early theme of "Digging" and later concerns. Line fragments referenced are found in Seamus Heaney's epitaph (from *The Gravel Walk*), his essay The Government of the Tongue, and poems: *The Journey Back, Tollund, Senior Infants*, and *The Riverbank Field* (original version from The Riverbank Field, 2007).

"Overtime and Charley" *I didn't expect to still be here...* was my father's lament at 87 years old during a recent visit in Florida where we spent a great deal of time watching the NCAA Tournament, which occasioned the "Overtime" series of poems.

"Ode to Interview Questions". My experience with interviews has been less than enjoyable, but I love the questions; they reveal so much about the person asking them and most of the answers I provide are subject and idiosyncratic (i.e. human).

"More Whiskey Please" is inspired by the occasioning argument of the Irish *Tain Bo Cuialnge*; the conflict arises when the two begin to compare their contributions as King and Queen *individually* to their marriage, and ultimately the Nation-state of Erin. The phrase *"friendly thighs"* is taken from Thomas Kinsella's translation of "The Tain".

"Lent Begins a Week Early". My father fell and fractured his hip while going out for a late lunch with his wife. He called from hospital asking if I would come to Florida to be with him. This happened the week before Lent, a time where I typically sacrifice a bad habit, take up a healthy discipline, or otherwise increasingly work to make the world a little better each day in an effort to live a more fulfilling Christian life.

"Dark Star Sapphire". When my father passed, of what little remained, he left us his personal effects. I have one of his rings, a dark star sapphire and when having extraordinary experiences, I will wear it and share the experience. It has become a totem; a sacred object, and symbol of my father's life.

Essay on Poetry

1.

When I pick-up and read a copy of most any current literary journal or poetry magazine, the first impression made is that *poetry* is many different things. There are prose poems, written in paragraph form. There are dislocated poems that move erratically over the page and leave the reader with a general sense of things. There are formal poems, familiarly recognizable. Poems paired with artwork to create an effect. Poetry that rhymes and poetry that don't. Some are just a few lines; others take several pages and are divided into sections. Some slowly find their way, others march, and then there are those that take long strides and leap their way down the page. I read a poem last month where parts of different lines had been erased, leaving only fragments that moved down the page – as if it were a lost poem by Sappho. There are seemingly as many types of poems as there are poets. And, isn't that the very nature of creation, that there is such great diversity within a given typology. Still, I am challenged to ask almost every time I read an anthology or poetry magazine, what is poetry?

I love poetry. Since I was a child it has engaged my imagination, and furthered my understanding of this life, and the world we share, in a most remarkable way. So I continue to read, cherish, and study poetry. Most of what I have learned in school through poetry endures, and is regularly tested and proven true- again. More still has been gained from my ongoing reading of poetry and literary journals and magazines, and even more from my attempts at writing poetry. Poetry is one of the few passions I can still indulge and not risk harm-unless one finds facing the truth or being neck deep in the beautiful harmful. Poetry is an essentially social phenomenon, as is human genius at its best. It is essentially relational and empathetic when reciprocal. Such is the nature of poetry.

When I was studying at The University of Michigan in 1984, Professor Russell Fraser defined poetry as, in its most basic sense, "bare bones language"; the idea being, like poetry itself, its definition should be in terms as concise as possible while conveying the fullest meaning. Later, in graduate studies at Oakland University, "runic" was the one word response that Professor Edward Haworth Hoeppner offered, as he trumped my two word understanding of poetry as a "durable relic." In my ongoing readings, Mary Oliver in her book *Rules for the Dance*[1] insightfully speaks of poetry as "breathing" and characterizes poetry as "statement." While Peter Quartermaine in his essay "Reading the Difficult"[2] considers poetry to be moments. These are just a few approaches to the question. Yet, from these basic, these whittled-down essential understandings of poetry, a dynamic emerges. Poetry is not one thing, it is the confluence of several; or, the way I see it, three.

First things inherently seem remedial; however poetry is first and foremost about language (i.e. words). Words (the right and best, old and new, familiar and unusual) are what poetry is about. Words that sound beautiful together or not, creating either mimetic or didactic awareness. Words that ripple with meaning,

---

[1] Oliver, Mary. *Rules for the Dance, A Handbook for Reading and Writing Metrical Verse*. Boston: Mariner Books, 1998.
[2] Quartermain, Peter. "Reading the Difficult." *Poetry*, October 2013.

confer inter-textual significance, or etymological importance. Words that have their singular import and character that no other word can signify. These are vital words; fresh, of their time, vigorous, and spill across the page with energy. There is a quality in poetry where if the word isn't right or best, if the sentiment lacks integrity, then the poem fails on a basic level. *Poetics* is the term I use when discussing the primacy of words in poetry. Here, in the emphasis on the primacy of words beyond mere meaning, Words chosen above all other words for many reasons. So, Poetry is part craft of the wordsmith-economist as distinctive from that of the prose writer.

Poetics would then also include, through and beyond word choice, the judicious use of poetic and linguistic conventions: sound, rhyme, meter, imagery, metaphor and simile, form, tone, etcetera. At its best, poetry flows and changes like breathing and this is manifest in the reading – how the poem reads, the form it takes, says as much about what it is expressing as do it's words. Poetry as a spoken medium, in its "orality", does not demand theatrics or undue emphasis to convey the poem; the inherent nature of the poem is manifest in its language, its words. How the words inform the poems meaning is a function of the poet's craft. Poetry is *the art of crafting words* into poetic language forms using poetic techniques. In both theory and practice, cognitively and viscerally, poetry functions to convey a meaning greater than the words it uses; and that is how the craft works. Through language, and often in a physical way, poetry shows us meaningful things about our humanity.

Poetry makes different demands on language. If I were writing an essay (like now), I would be working with sentences as my basic unit of thought and building paragraphs with them to convey a more complete sense of meaning. Not so with poetry. While poetry is as concerned with complete thoughts and clear meanings as prose (and therefore needs to be as good as prose), poetry's basic unit of thought is not the sentence... but *the line*. Poetry is written in lines, each of which should be as good as the next. Each line carries its equal share of weight in relation to the others, and the poem holds with the integrity of what Robert Frost characterizes as a silk tent in the wind on shifting beach sands. The silken tent, although supple, is not a fragile structure, but durable and sturdy as it redistributes the stress of wind and shifting sands. Supple. Sturdy. Durable. Lines become stanzas, which group lines that belong together and break to indicate a shift, advancement or retraction, as the poem works its way to fulfillment.

So, poetry represents a structure (a tent, lodge, house or castle; or a tree) and bears a similar physical integrity whether organic or artificial. Poems, too, possess a design, an architecture, which is frequently organic and works intentionally. For the foundations of poems and buildings are each laid early, and inform the scope and character of their work. The structure, or form, either informs or detracts from the landscape. Successful works possess forms that are harmonious with their content. Forms such as sonnets, villanelles, sestinas, and rhymed line stanzas are as significant and telling. These shorter form poems are often comprised of a singular sentence or idea, a singular stanza, advancing on itself, and often transform into a fresh or unanticipated perspective on its subject. Long free-form poems, like *Leaves of Grass* by Walt Whitman[3], unmetered and unrhymed, can be equally harmonious

---

[3] Whitman, Walt. *Leaves of Grass.* Ed. Jason Stacy. Iowa City: University of Iowa Press, 1860.

and satisfying as those poems working within more formal constraints. Within the long pastoral lines and many stanzas of longer free-form poems are complete thoughts, sentences and sentence fragments, which serve to clarify and inform in ways that a short form poem simply cannot. Essentially though, when attempting to understand poetry in its most basic element, we are working with lines; the poetic line.

Secondly, poetry is about the subject of the poem, that which the poem conveys, or what I consider to be the *Poem*. This would be Moments, humanity's runes, the event that occasions poetry (the death of a loved one, a sparrow, or a world leader; all love poems; the changing of the seasons; war; a morning bus ride or a red wheelbarrow). These events, both extraordinary and every day common, are poetic *moments* where the human sensibility engages at a deeper level and comprehends a truth or beauty that is more immediate, more clear, more harmoniously experienced, organically engendered and perceptively pure, than regular speech can express. Show me Love. Show me God. Show me Faith. Show me Beauty and Truth. Show me love, again (there are so many different types, and they evolve in the most wonderful and unanticipated ways). This is why the "objective correlative", as T.S. Eliot first wrote in his 1919 essay on *Hamlet*[4], is still relevant if not central in poetry. Poetry recognizes and responds to humanity's unique and otherwise inexpressible, or marginally expressible, experience with clarity and economy.

All truths are by their nature essential and many essential truths become cliché or maxim (as such these "truths" become devalued in expression that is trite and

---

[4] Eliot, T.S. "Hamlet", *Selected Essays*. London: Faber and Faber: 1932.

stale). So, here it is important to differentiate poetic moments in regard to Truth. What I speak of are the smaller human moments of truth and not "god moments," although the truth poets encounter even if with a small "t" is often large and formative. A "god moment" is that particular point where what we perceive as "God" enters into our lives and everything is changed (through His will, not ours). While human moments and god moments may appear in opposition, they are often complimentary. Human moments, the moments that poets write from, are those moments where the poet's sensibility and perceptive of our humanity is brought into a crisp focus and clarity in a way (poetic) that could not be arrived at otherwise.

Either way, recognition of the confluence found in moments is central to the poetic sensibility. Sometimes our awareness of these moments is discovered in an ordinary event, sometimes it is a force majeure that serves to be transformative, still other times it is a confluence of little events that repeat until we perceive a larger significance. Often a relationship emerges which occasions the poem. (Stare into the void long enough and the void will stare back.) The act of writing poetry occasionally elicits poems about poetry just as the act of creating lends insight into creation. Poems are woven out of the materials at hand, either imaginative and/or experientially factual; it is where we clearly discern the beautiful and the true.

Both internally and externally occurring, these moments reveal our humanity- often in surprising ways. Whatever the truth of our human condition may be, in our recognition and response, and expand our understanding. Such understanding of our humanity is inherently subjective knowledge gained from the experience of being fully, and often imperfectly, human:

Our way, not His. My experience is that, at our human best, religion and the arts fundamentally align to the mutual benefit of humanity and creation. (Of course, the Creator of Creation has expressed his will to us repeatedly over time as recorded in our histories and arts. The question, as always, is do we hear it and do we care?)

And, lastly, the third element involved in defining what poetry is, is *the poet as individual progenitor and personality of their time*: the idiosyncratic manner of language (idiom) and artistic perspective as they relate to the individual poet/artist. Poetry is not constantly being reinvented and redefined through the individual interests of writers; instead, it evolves like a dialogue across time and within various traditions. Virgil rests heavily on the *Odyssey* by Homer for the telling of his *Aeneid* (they are essentially the same story from different perspectives), yet they are by sensibility told quiet differently. Of course, Shakespeare is recognizably Shakespeare, despite the volumes that he wrote, and is not to be confused with Alexander Pope, John Milton, or Sir Thomas Wyatt. And, often, poets over time borrow from and build on those influences that they, either technically or by sensibility, value. Walt Whitman in his evolution of the line and pastoral voice seemingly owes a debt to William Wordsworth. Likewise, contemporary poets (those who are contemporaries) will distinguish themselves both stylistically and by voice. Consider how Robert Frost and Wallace Stevens share similar contemporary poetic concerns yet they are distinctly different – as are W.S. Merwin, John Ashbury, Seamus Heaney and Donald Hall.

The poet is engaged in a conversation greater than that experienced through poem alone. This conversation reflects not only the individual interests of the poet, but their cultural propensities and concerns – whether local or global, personal or political, material or spiritual. The Western literary tradition, for practical reasons to be discussed later, is largely influenced by Judeo-Christian thought, especially in America despite its insistence on multiculturalism and secular institutions with the separation of church and state. However, as in any relationship influence runs both ways, and the American Catholic-Christian church is equally influenced by poets and poetry. Cardinal J. Henry Newman observes "with Christians, a poetical view of things is a duty. We are bid to color all things with hues of faith, to see a divine meaning in every event."[5] The presence of God as experienced in the human moment; where His will and ours not only align, but become one.

Inclusion, not exclusion, serves as my motivation in answering the question, *what is poetry?* There are good poems, great poems, marginal poems, and those that need to be "re-visioned". And, poetry as a branch of literature responds to cultural influences and traditions. Reading poetry, all poetry, in its great range and diversity is essential toward understanding what poetry is. To this end, anthologies and literary journals are nearly indispensable. Yet, it is more important to be aware of and versed in traditions of poetry, as well as the poets that have contributed to the larger conversation over time (*sic* another T.S. Eliot essay, *Tradition and the Individual Talent*).[6] Within the long standing conversation that poetry evokes, veins of thought, blood-lines of poetic traditions can be

---

[5] Newman, John Henry. *Poetry, with reference to Aristotle's Poetics*. Boston: Ginn & Company, 1891.

[6] Eliot, T.S. "Tradition and the Individual Talent", *Selected Essays*. London: Faber and Faber: 1932.

identified and arguments for diverse understandings made. My understanding of poetry begins broadly with the Western literary tradition, which finds its roots in Greek and Latin writings, then follows the English language poets, and narrows (for better or worse) to the contemporary American scene, which at times I find chaotic.

2.

Despite my appreciation of creation's diversity, I find myself returning to my roots every few years as if to stay anchored in a steady stream of new ideas about poetry and trends in criticism. My roots are deep roots. They are anchored in the durable and supple English language poems, in memorable rhymed and metered verse first published in medieval times when the oral tradition found a home in the written word. Here, forms that vary in style flourish. Just as there is not simply one type of maple tree, or trout, or human, poems share the same qualities that classify them as poetry. The first poem Professor Russell Fraser had our English class analyze was (and is) most telling, and continues today for me to be most satisfying (although in my ongoing readings I enjoy the anonymous verse of Medieval scribes and poet scholars written in their dialects as much if not more). The course was titled, tongue in check by Professor Fraser, "A Brief History of the Short Poem," and the first named poet we studied was Thomas Wyatt the Elder. Sir Thomas Wyatt (1503-1542) wrote a lifetime before William Shakespeare (1564-1616) began his career, and authored one of my favorite poems, the sonnet, "Whoso List to Hunt":[7]

> Whoso list to hunt, I know where is a hind,
> But as for me, alas, I may no more.
> The vain travail hath wearied me so sore,
> I am of them that farthest cometh behind.
> Yet may I by no means my wearied mind
> Draw from the deer, but as she fleeth afore
> Fainting I follow. I leave off therefore,
> Since in a net I seek to hold the wind.
> Who list her hunt, I put him out of doubt,
> As well as I may spend his time in vain.
> And graven with diamonds in letters plain
> There is written, her fair neck round about:
> *Noli me tangere*, for Caesar's I am,
> And wild for to hold, though I seem tame. (1-14)

I will spare you my interpretation and analysis; however, it is recognizably a Petrarchan (or Italian) sonnet, the earliest sonnet form, popularized before the advent of the printing press, and decidedly a love poem. Distinctly steeped in Western culture and traditions, the poem moves from pure desire to fleeting love, love unrequited, love divine: Poetry for adults only, and one so hot as to be the cause much speculation about the subject or object of the poem. Certainly such beauty could only be the fairest in all of England and royalty, royal property, the Queen herself! Sir Thomas Wyatt was nearly interred in London Tower for this most extraordinary and evocative love sonnet, which is the last place you wanted to be as it would likely be the last place you ever saw.

---

[7] Wyatt, Thomas. "Whoso List to Hunt." In *Songes and Sonettes Written by the Ryght honorable Lord Henry Howard, late Earle of Surrey, and others*. London: 1557.

Here, perhaps, is the first divergence in answer to the question what is poetry: Where do we, as an audience for poetry, claim our roots? While matters of cultural diversity are considerable, all poetry shares similar characteristics, as do all trees, fish or people. Ultimately, our understanding largely depends on the tradition of poetry that we as readers are exposed to and enjoy. Our first and most unadulterated impressions are often most true and enduring. Regardless of our cultural imperatives, as children in our family nurseries or institutional daycare centers we were read to, and read, children's poems; poems that are often short, rhyming, clever verses that tell nonsensical stories. These nursery rhymes have song-like and narrative qualities, and have been shared, cherished and adored for generations so that they have become part of popular culture. These are often the first poems we encounter and the first we share with our own children. Who hasn't joyfully recited as an adult their favorite classic? Mine is...

> Hey, diddle, diddle,
> The cat and the fiddle,
> The cow jumped over the moon.
> The little dog laughed,
> To see such sport,
> And the dish ran away with the spoon. [8]

Who knows exactly when, who, or under what circumstances this children's verse, which plays off of similar 16th century verse, was written? Not Wikipedia! What we do know for certain is that these lines have held the test of time as all great poetry does. Although small and playful, they are memorable. Cats that fiddle,

---

[8] "Hey Diddle, Diddle." In *Favorite Nursery Rhymes from Mother Goose,* 57. Seymour: The Greenwich Workshop Press. 2007.

dogs that laugh, jumping cows, animated tableware! This is a moment of pure joy. It is a celebration of successfully reconciling unlikely, improbable and disparate things; of reconciling ourselves with a large, unwieldy and often threatening universe. We laugh to think dogs our equals, cows have supernatural powers, cats possess extraordinary artistic capacities or that the inanimate can suddenly come to life and exercise willfulness. These lines engage the imagination and speak to our humanity at a level beyond the literal, the political and the theological. And, they are a durable relic of a Western culture whose literature is constantly being revised and expanded upon.

Many years after leaving the nursery, as a college graduate, the first poetry reading that I hunted down tickets for and took myself to, and Joanne (it was a date), was amazing. It was held at Hill Auditorium in Ann Arbor in 1985 and featured poets Galway Kinnell, Donald Hall, Seamus Heaney and a farmer from Kentucky, Wendell Berry. It is one of those nights that can, and should, never be forgotten. By the end of the evening, it was Seamus Heaney that I gained an appreciation for and would follow intently for the next thirty years, while Wendell Berry receded into the shadows until being rediscovered nearly fifteen years later. Hall and Kinnell would remain favorites and followed with interest.

Anyhow, I was most familiar (and enamored) at the time with Galway Kinnell's poems and went hoping to hear him read my favorite at the time, "The Bear",[9] a long, meta-poetic, poem detailing a dream of hunting, then becoming, a bear. The poem opens with an examination of bear scat while tracking the bear and

[9] Kinnell, Galway. "The Bear." In *Three Books,* 67-70. New York: Houghton Mifflin Company. 2002

concludes by posing the question all poets must answer for themselves: "what, anyway,/ was that sticky infusion, that rank flavor of blood, that poetry, by which I lived?" Even truth, when found in a bloody stool, can be beautiful if cast in the proper (playfully reflexive) light.

While Galway Kinnell has several poems that share this meta-poetic quality that conveys his sense of poetry, engaging in poetry as the subject of poems has a long tradition which serves to illustrate the essential nature of poetry. Perhaps the oldest poem in which this concern for poetry, a self-awareness of the poet in the act of creating and seeking to understand poetry (self-reflexive), that I am familiar with is "Pangur Ban," a poem written in Gaelic in the margin of a Latin text being transcribed by an anonymous monk in ninth century Ireland. I like Robin Flower's translation best as it captures a humbly direct and sometimes playful spirit of the anonymous author, and it closely matches the original couplet rhyme scheme and line length. It is a poem that begins self-reflectively and resolves in an understanding of poetry that transcends.

Pangur Ban (from the Irish by Robin Flower)

I and Pangur Ban my cat,
'Tis a like task we are at:
Hunting mice is his delight,
Hunting words I sit all night.

Better far than praise of men
'Tis to sit with book and pen;
Pangur bears me no ill-will,
He too plies his simple skill.

'Tis a merry task to see
At our tasks how glad are we,

When at home we sit and find
Entertainment to our mind.

Oftentimes a mouse will stray
In the hero Pangur's way;
Oftentimes my keen thought set
Takes a meaning in its net.

'Gainst the wall he sets his eye
Full and fierce and sharp and sly;
'Gainst the wall of knowledge I
All my little wisdom try.

When a mouse darts from its den,
O how glad is Pangur then!
O what gladness do I prove
When I solve the doubts I love!

So in peace our task we ply,
Pangur Ban, my cat, and I;
In our arts we find our bliss,
I have mine and he has his.

Practice every day has made
Pangur perfect in his trade;
I get wisdom day and night
Turning darkness into light.

Poetry, in an early self-reflexive sense, is a playful act for the overt purpose of gaining wisdom through enlarged perspective, is largely informed through early works preserved in the Latin tradition—and is transformative. Bear in mind that the history, literature, philosophy, science and arts (the culture) of Western civilization was preserved in texts assimilated and generated by the great Roman Empire. And, from the Fall of the Roman Empire, which began around 300 AD, until the emergence of the university system and printing press, the texts that survived the Middle Ages were preserved largely by private libraries and the Roman Catholic Church, which for over a century is largely credited with transcribing and maintaining these documents. These were the Dark Ages. During this time in Europe, and especially Ireland at its far border, hundreds of years would pass and little if anything would change. Life around 900 AD at Reichenau Abbey, where scribes worked diligently preserving texts daily, was substantially the same as it was in 600 AD.

However, the re-emergence of the university system in Europe, as established by the Jesuit Order of the Catholic Church in Paris (1160-1200), served to recapture and preserve the wealth of literature and history that had been scattered and ravaged during the Dark Ages. Then, the invention of the printing press by Gutenberg at Mainz, Germany (c1450a.d.) allowed for the rapid distribution of what had been lost to Western civilization during the Middle Ages, and a renaissance in the arts and sciences. Religious texts, histories, medical works, technical manuals and the classics were being translated and produced at a rate that far exceeded the hand copying methods that had been employed for thousands of years. In a matter of a couple hundred years there were contemporary works being exchanged with a passion and a newfound freedom (within the confines of political and religious governance). In these "early" new works we see the ongoing concerns and impact of poetry. In 1648, Robert Herrick published a book of his poetry, 1400 poems in all, among them is "Delight in Disorder."[10]

---

[10] Williams, John & F. Egelsfield, Publishers. "Delight in Disorder." In *Hesperides: Or, The Works Both Humane & Divine of Robert Herrick Esq.* London: 1648.

A sweet disorder in the dress
Kindles in clothes a wantonness;
A lawn about the shoulders thrown
Into a fine distraction;
An erring lace, which here and there
Enthrals the crimson stomacher;
A cuff neglectful, and thereby
Ribands to flow confusedly;
A winning wave, deserving note,
In the tempestuous petticoat;
A careless shoe-string, in whose tie
I see a wild civility:
Do more bewitch me, than when art
Is too precise in every part.

Although less runic and overtly meta-poetic, it speaks to the same artful concerns expressed in "Pangur Ban." Here, language is considered as dress. But, dress for *what?* Dress for thoughts, ideas, feelings, history, God, the naked play of the imagination? The verse is freer in meter, but the lyric qualities of end rhyme persist. The freedom expressed comes at a time where the oral tradition of poetry is finding a new home in the printed word and, while rhyme is still a recognizable aspect of poetry, the written word allows certain liberties in other structural techniques less closely aligned with song.

Lastly, consider as a corollary the contemporary English sonnet by Robert Frost (1874-1963), "The Silken Tent," [11] which I have previously mentioned. Here, the poem is a single thought and a single sentence, which, like a tent pole, acts as a center that supports everything that flows around and flutters in the wind.

---

[11] Frost, Robert. "The Silken Tent." *A Witness Tree.* 1942.

As I reach the last line of the poem I am left asking, what are we talking about here: a woman, a tent, a poem? Regardless, the poem is a physical structure and mediated response to our understanding of the human condition.

> She is as in a field a silken tent
> At midday when the sunny summer breeze
> Has dried the dew and all its ropes relent,
> So that in guys it gently sways at ease,
> And its supporting central cedar pole,
> That is its pinnacle to heavenward
> And signifies the sureness of the soul,
> Seems to owe naught to any single cord,
> But strictly held by none, is loosely bound
> By countless silken ties of love and thought
> To everything on earth the compass round,
> And only by one's going slightly taut
> In the capriciousness of summer air
> Is of the slightest bondage made aware.

The poem analogously shows the relationship of form and content in achieving integrity of structure, albeit an otherwise humble silken tent. As the written word has taken a more prominent role in poetry over the past five hundred years, poetry begins to increasingly possess discursive qualities that convey complex metaphoric and analogous meanings. Poetry is no longer merely song to be chanted for entertainment around the table. As Frost concludes, awareness (and I suggest a heightened awareness of subject matter and meaning) has become central to poetry. Poetry, even overtly rhyming sonnets, may still delight, but poetic verse is no longer concerned with "diddling." The very act of writing poetry and confining it to the page begins to pervade poetic works. Consequently, the subject of the poems reflects a continued evolution of poetic expression; the delight experienced by heightened awareness, the palpable excitement of self-reflexive and meta-poetic moments, a loosening but not a loss of formal constraints—of structure –in favor of organic expression and the subsequent emergence of the poet within the poem: *persona ex machine*, person from/in the machine.

And, isn't that also the very nature of creation that even within great diversity we see the impress of the Creator, the essence of the creative force. How can there be creation without a Creator? Here comes the awareness that we in our humanity are a part of the diversity. We are animus *and* spiritus; human animal imbued with a spirit, a soulfulness, distinctly different from the rest of animal creation. We create structures not of necessity, but of a conceptualized want. As we stand against the darkness, a darkness where our imaginations conceive specters of animated dinnerware and supernatural cows, we seek relationship with other soulful beings. The want for relationship, which all religion and cultures identify as the motivation our Creator had for bringing us into being. Within the forms and structures of poetry, we find not only integrity of meaning and a deeper understanding of our humanity, but the perceptive presence of a creative force— if not an appreciation of and shared experience with, the Creator.

3.

So, *what is poetry?* A better approach to understanding the question may be to consider what is *not* poetry? Poetry is not religion, not science, not history, not philosophy, not medicine despite its restorative properties. Poetry is not simply the statement of a truth or the pleasing expression of sounds. Poetry is not just a matter of forms or systems of language. Poetry is not prose. Poetry is inclusive and distinct from these many complimentary schools and disciplines. We can find all within the universe of poetry, yet the character of poetry is different. And, its distinctive character informs its unique function. That poems endure as some of civilizations earliest literary artifacts, suggests that poems are inherently useful and valuable relics.

More to the point, what is the function of poetry? Or, better still, how does poetry function? In my search for an essential understanding, I (like many others) attempt to reconcile poetry's history, tradition, critical underpinnings and theoretic basis', I have gone back as far as is reasonably accessible in Western literature and within the context of my traditions.

And, Like most, my journey begins with the *Ars Poetica* (yes, Latin for the "Art of Poetry") by Horace. Here, Truth and Beauty are first considered central to poetry. For nearly two-thousand years, the measure of poetry in Western civilization was based on Beauty and Truth. Poetry functioned as an arbiter of what and how humanity engaged with (perceived, thought of, found) Truth and Beauty. Today those elements are still largely upheld as a basis for Poetry, although they are continually being challenged. The issue today is that truth has been devalued, and is spelled with a lower case "t", as it has become a matter of perspective. Truth, it seems, has lost its absolute authority in contemporary society in favor of lesser, changing, perceptive truths. Truth has become a form of entertainment in popular (civilized and educated) culture and has resulted in an abundance of contemporary poetry, which employs numerous and diverse schools of critical thought, building a literary

Tower of Babel in regard to Truth. Religions will still tell us Truths and Philosophy will argue and advocate Truths; however, poetry today seeks to provide an objective correlative to show humanity's larger truths through smaller moments that become almost inexpressively expansive, or conversely to take the nearly inexpressively expansive and condense it into the poet's essential, perceptive, experience.

The American poet, Emily Dickinson, advises; "Tell all the truth but tell it slant--".

Tell All the Truth[12]

Tell all the Truth but tell it slant—
Success in Circuit lies
To bright for our infirm delight
The Truth's superb surprise
As lightning to the Children eased
With explanation kind
The Truth must dazzle gradually
Or everyman be blind—

Truth (all the truth) illuminates, like the sun. And, like the sun, its light is slant as it passes through the atmosphere and into the poets' window. You don't want to look directly at the Truth for too long, much like you don't want to stare at or spend too much time in the sun as it can damage your sight, or drive you mad. A perspective slant is essential for handling the Truth. The perceptive slant that poets offer provides their distinctive voice and sensibility as it engages and illuminates. And, to go one step further, whereas there are meditatively reflective and self-reflective qualities present in poetry as it pursues the Truth, the essential

---

[12] Dickinson, Emily. "Tell All the Truth."

quality of the poets' sensibility is refractive if not circuitous. The poetic sensibility is atmospheric for the poets' world. This relationship between the poet, the poem (inherent truth/beauty) and poetry (language and linguistic expression) is central to my understanding of poetry. Poetry's Truth is a truth that transcends reason and argument characterized by mere prose, a Truth manifest in an economy of language that is didactic and mimetic- denotative and connotative – as it conveys the fullest sense with leveraged economy. As such, it is a perceptive approach that regards both small truths and absolute Truth with similar critical and idiomatic fervor.

Whatever truth poetry conveys, it conveys with the slant of the poets perspective. In my experience, this perspective slant which engenders a greater awareness of our humanity is delightfully playful. Seeing things as and in other things is a fundamental form of animated play which takes me back to my childhood and early love of poetry- but I digress. More importantly, this playfulness of perspective is as a function of the poetic sensibility. This perspective is contemporaneous with the poets' expanding awareness. As such, it often represents a fresh (if not imperfect) insight into our humanity as experienced in time, and surprises in unlikely ways. Poetry then represents the truth of humanity's sensibility as it evolves in the act of refracting. How Wallace Stevens views death in his poem "Anecdote of the Jar" is as beautiful and shares as much integrity as how John Keats similarly reflected in his "Ode on a Grecian Urn". Each is of their time and brings a distinct perspective slant- and each is beautifully wrought.

And, what of Beauty? Has Beauty also lost its way. Has Beauty been devalued by the subjective whims of fashion and critics? There have been many iterations of the phrase *beauty is in the eye of the beholder* from Shakespeare in *Love's Labour Lost* (2.1.15), to present-day pop culture icons. Still, beyond these subjective measures of beauty, there is affirmed to be an absolute beauty that the human sensibility responds to in nature. The earliest attributable mention to an absolute beauty I am aware of is that of Plato: "Remember how in that communion only, beholding beauty with the eye of the mind, he will be enabled to bring forth, not images of beauty, but realities (for he has hold not of an image but of a reality), and bringing forth and nourishing true virtue to become the friend of God and be immortal, if mortal man may."[13] Beauty, inherent beauty, is absolute. During the Renaissance in Europe, this inherent quality found in the Beautiful was quantified in the Golden Rule of art and architecture where proportion and integrity are esteemed by the human eye, as harmony is by the ear.

In the visual arts, beauty is found in the use of color and texture that create movement and convey mood, tone and feeling. Artists, like poets, illuminate their subject with light (both natural and artificial), which slants, casts shadows and sometimes reflectively bursts from the canvas. Contemporary poetry is most like Impressionism as it allows room for the audience's imagination to engage with the poem and explore the moment, bringing their own experience and perspectives to bear. John Keats, in letters to his brother, after viewing an exhibit of Claude Monet's impressionist paintings, referred to this technique of engagement as *negative capability*. In other words, the artist rendering the impression gives enough information to form a general understanding, and

---

[13] Plato, *The Symposium.* Translated by Christopher Gill. Harmondsworth: Penguin Books, 1999.

leaves negative space for the audience to fill in with their own imagination/impression (Is that dark smudge on the water, a boat in the distance, a log, or what is... *that*?). We enter into the artist's work and are active participants in discovering beauty.

Still I ask, with Truth devalued, is Beauty now also under siege? The most recent Art Prize in Grand Rapids, Michigan, de-emphasized Beauty as criteria for judging art. Let us look at art without an eye for that which is subjectively beautiful. Where is the integrity in art, if it is not responsive to the human sensibility? Many cultures and traditions place value on the beautiful simply for the delight it provides, and perhaps you can think of a maxim that you adhere to. Here I would echo the sentiment of Pope Paul VI: *The world in which we live needs beauty in order not to sink into despair.* Beauty becomes more than a subjective opinion, it serves as a manifestation of perspective that transforms the everyday ordinary and mundane into the extraordinary- an approach the creative takes toward expanding our understanding. Why we need beauty may be a specious topic for another essay, as need is perhaps the wrong word; however, that we in our condition are attracted to, if not compelled toward, the beautiful, the delightful, the wondrous, the inescapably shiny and ebullient, is a material and sensory fact of our humanity.

Both Truth and Beauty are found in the form a poem takes and the content of the poetry as idiomatically expressed by the poet. Here, the Poem is a contemporaneously expressed truth that makes all Love poems original, reflections on death fresh and the familiar mysteries of the unknown new. Here, what is beautiful is what is envisioned and shared by the poet in the poet's characteristic way. The poetics employed (metaphors and similes, rhyme, line length, imagery, statements and analogies, etc.), the sounds and images words elicit, work together and against one another to reconcile an understanding greater than the words alone could ever express. Ralph Waldo Emerson, a contemporary of Emily Dickinson's and member of the Enlightenment Movement of the mid-1800's, states in his essay *The Poet*, "A man is half his words, the other half is his expression."[14] These two fundamental aspects of communication combine in poetry to create a truth and beauty greater than their individual parts. Here perception and sensibility are meted out through a characteristic approach to language. This dynamic creates additional complexities and considerations today when answering the question, what is poetry?

Today, poetic considerations involve critical approaches to *expression* (both language/linguistics and perception/point-of-view), which were acknowledged over three hundred years ago. By the turn of the eighteenth century John Dryden, in his preface to *Fables, Ancient and Modern*[15], first draws the analogy of poet as builder ("'Tis with a Poet as with a Man that designs to build, and is very exact..."), then expands on the central concerns of poetry by adding *clarity* and *freshness of language* as criteria (tools of the trade), especially in regard to translations: "When an ancient Word for its Sound and Significancy deserves to be revived, I have that reasonable Veneration for Antiquity, to restore it... Words are not like Land-marks, so sacred as never to be removed: Customs are chang'd, and even Statues are silently repeal'd, when the Reason ceases

---

[14] Emerson, Ralph Waldo. "The Poet." In *Essays: Second Series.* 1844.

[15] Dryden, John. *Fables, Ancient and Modern, Translated into verse from Homer, Ovid, Boccace, & Chaucer: with Original Poems.* London: 1700.

for which they were enacted." Breathing new life into classic works written in dead languages that survived the fall of empires, plagues, paradigmatic shifts in economic/political/social thought – not to mention the natural disasters and the decay of time – is most noble and just.

However, as Dryden observes, tastes and audiences change, and the poet responds and adapts as "He alters his Mind as the work proceeds... So (in translating ancient texts) it has happened to me." Dryden's veneration and desire to restore ancient texts led him at times by his own admission to take latitudes with the poetry for Beauty's sake (as the fashion of such changes demands) and to make occasional omissions for reasons of moral consideration. More than simply adding a freshness of language and clarity, translations therefore can result in shifts of meaning due to the evolution of linguistic, historical, political, religious or critical schools of thought. Such indulgence has nearly become the national past-time today. Conversely there have been extraordinary re-discoveries, as meanings are captured that long ago were abandoned. *What* was being said in translation becomes as important as *how* it was said, as the poetic line evolves with the written word from songlike rhyme and metered verse to freer verse and prose poems.

So, *what is Poetry?* Artifact? Truth? Beauty? Clarity? Confluence? Reciprocity? Empathetic phenomenal verse? A silken tent on a beach or scat on the trail? Certainly it is the relationship between language, form and the Poet; the relationship between what is being said, how it is being said and who is saying it. More than that in its playfully perspective character, poetry is a; *Hey, diddle, diddle... turning darkness into light... a careless shoe-string, in who's tie/ I see a wild civility... since in a net I seek to hold the wind... the sureness of the soul... that sticky effusion, that rank flavor of blood....* And, whereas this is an essay and not a poem, I assert that poetry is an organically engendered harmonious confluence where humanity's beauty and truth emerge in a clear and concise idiom manifest in lines. One day, while writing a poem, I too may self-reflexively turn meta-poetic and thus arrive at an understanding that will harden like amber, capture my sense of the poem in the offing, refract an imperfect s ant of light, and represent the beautiful in a fresh "soundscape" that can only be poetry.

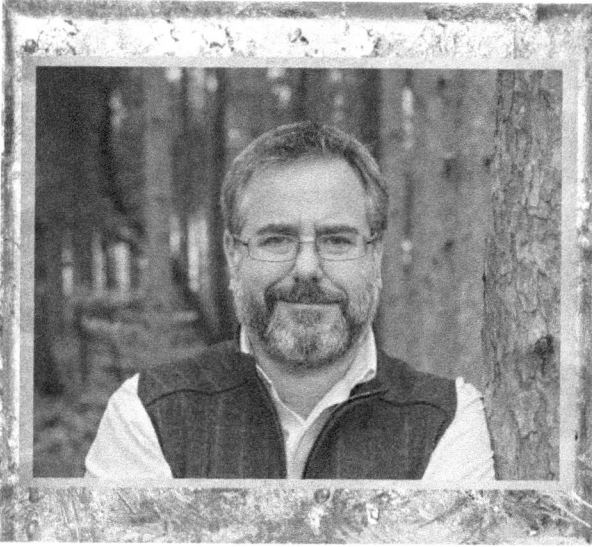

Michael D. Jones

A business professional, poet, and father of four, Michael Jones is the author of two collections of poems with numerous accolades and two Pushcart Prize nominated poems; Lady (Unlikely Trees, 2014) and Ambersong (Kerf, 2015).

Since publishing his first collection *The Patter of Bare Feet (1998)* in an anthology of Michigan writers, Michael Jones has won awards for his poetry throughout Michigan. *Unlikely Trees* is his second collection poems; they expose a mind that knows itself, a sensibility that is associative and relational, and they offer a perspective that indulges in the wondrous and miraculous - sometimes with delight, sometimes not. He has a Master of Arts degree in English from Oakland University, and a Bachelor of Arts degree in English and Communications from the University of Michigan. He and his wife, Joanne, live and work in Holland, MI.

www.michaeljonesmipoet.com

Also written by Michael D. Jones:

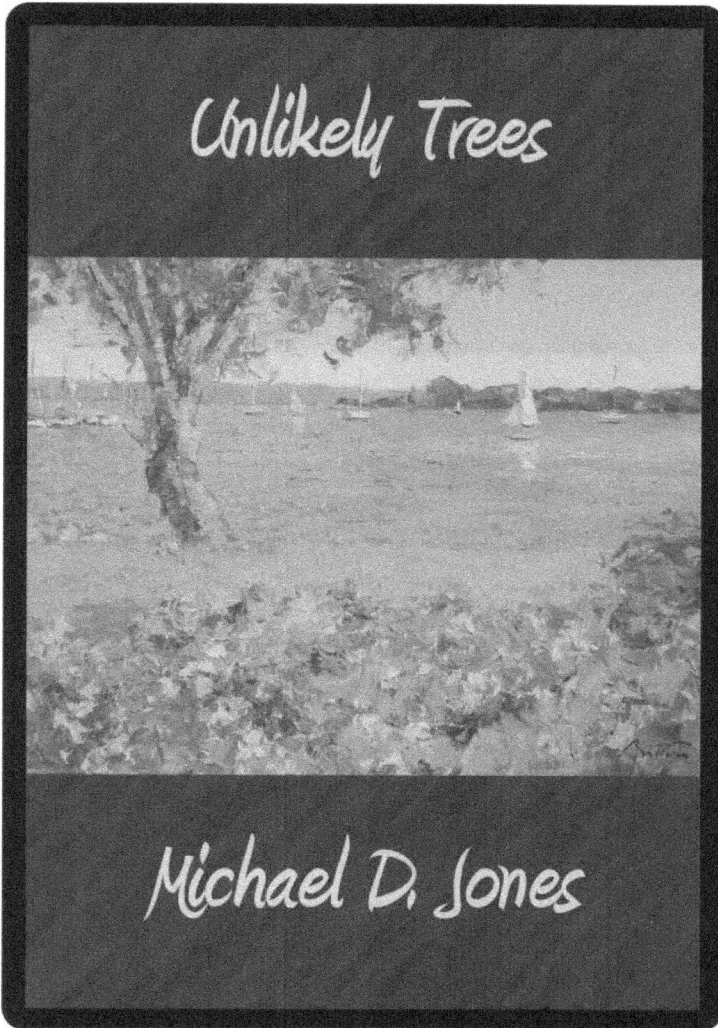

Available in Print on Amazon.com and in E-book Kindle format.

www.ingramcontent.com/pod-product-compliance
Lightning Source LLC
Chambersburg PA
CBHW031570040426
42445CB00009B/271